W9-BAA-746

Creative Crafts for Kids

Birthday CRAFTS

By Greta Speechley

Gareth Stevens
Publishing

Please visit our Web site www.garethstevens.com. For a free color catalog of all our high-quality books, call toll free 1-800-542-2595 or fax 1-877-542-2596.

Library of Congress Cataloging-in-Publication Data
Speechley, Greta, 1948-
    Birthday crafts / Greta Speechley.
      p. cm. -- (Creative crafts for kids)
    Includes index.
    ISBN 978-1-4339-3552-7 (library binding) -- ISBN 978-1-4339-3553-4 (pbk.)
    ISBN 978-1-4339-3554-1 (6-pack)
    1. Handicraft--Juvenile literature. 2. Birthday parties--Juvenile literature. I. Title.
  TT160.S655 2010
  745.594'1--dc22   2009037145

Published in 2010 by
Gareth Stevens Publishing
111 East 14th Street, Suite 349
New York, NY 10003

© 2010 The Brown Reference Group Ltd.

For Gareth Stevens Publishing:
Art Direction: Haley Harasymiw
Editorial Direction: Kerri O'Donnell

For The Brown Reference Group Ltd:
Editorial Director: Lindsey Lowe
Managing Editor: Tim Harris
Children's Publisher: Anne O'Daly
Design Manager: David Poole
Production Director: Alastair Gourlay

Picture Credits:
All photographs: Martin Norris
Front Cover: Shutterstock: Perry Correll and Martin Norris

Manufactured in the United States of America
1 2 3 4 5 6 7 8 9   12 11 10   172-9312

CPSIA compliance information: Batch #BRW0102GS: For further information contact Gareth Stevens, New York, New York at 1-800-542-2595.

Contents

Introduction

This book is packed with everything you need to throw a brilliant birthday party. Make the Splat invites from paper plates, then get to work decorating the house for the big day. There is an ice-cream cone door knocker to make and balloons covered in glittery swirls. Have fun and Happy Birthday!

YOU WILL NEED

Each project includes a list of all the things you need.

Before you go out and buy lots of new materials, have a look around at home to see what you could use instead. For example, you can cut cardboard shapes out of cereal boxes.

You can buy air-drying clay and craft foam from a craft shop and other items, such as paper plates and rubber gloves, from a department store. You will need to buy hard, colorful candies for the Snack stand on page 8 and soft candies for the Candy chain on page 6.

Getting started

 Read the steps for the project first.

 Gather together all the items you need.

 Cover your work surface with newspaper.

 Wear an apron, or change into old clothes.

A message for adults

All the projects in Birthday Crafts have been designed for children to make, but occasionally they will need you to help. Some of the projects do require the use of sharp utensils, such as scissors or needles. Please read through the instructions before your child starts work.

Making patterns

Follow these steps to make the patterns on pages 30 and 31. Using a pencil, trace the pattern onto tracing paper. To cut the pattern out of cardboard, turn the tracing over, and lay it onto the cardboard. Rub firmly over the pattern with a pencil. The shape will appear on the cardboard. Cut it out. To use a half pattern, trace the shape once, then flip over the tracing paper, and trace again to complete the whole shape. Or follow the instructions for the project.

When you have finished

 Wash paintbrushes, and put everything away.

 Put pens, pencils, paints, and glue in an old box or ice-cream container.

 Keep scissors and any other sharp items in a safe place.

 Stick needles and pins into a pincushion or a piece of scrap cloth.

BE SAFE

Look out for the safety boxes. They will appear whenever you need to ask an adult for help.

 Ask an adult to help you use sharp scissors.

Candy chain

Make a beautiful locket for your birthday that shows how old you are. The chain is made out of candies, so you can eat them up when you take it off at the end of the day.

YOU WILL NEED

candies	scrap paper
needle and thread	scissors
pink, green, blue, and white air-drying clay (harden in the oven)	clay cutter
	round pencil

1 Mix up blue and white clay to make a swirly pastel blue clay. Roll it out using a round pencil. Mix green and white to make pale green clay and pink and white to make pale pink clay.

2 Draw a small heart onto paper, and cut it out. Lay it on the pale blue clay. Cut around the paper template using a clay cutter.

6

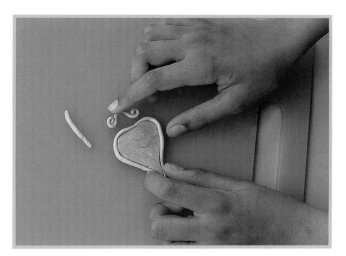

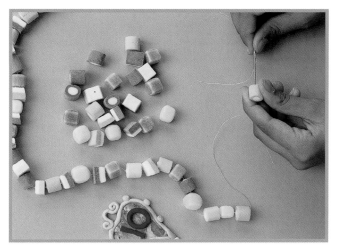

3 Roll out a thin sausage of pink clay. Wrap it around the heart to make a frame. Make a second thin sausage of pink clay, and twist it into a loop to go on top of the heart so you can thread the heart onto a chain.

4 Roll tiny balls of pale green clay to press around the edge of the heart. Roll sausages of blue clay, and shape them into your age. Press them onto the heart. Use a needle to thread cotton through candies to make the chain.

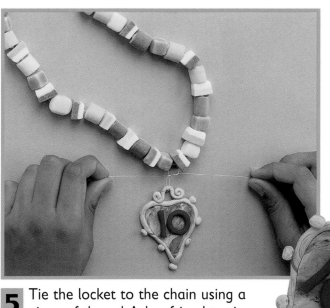

5 Tie the locket to the chain using a piece of thread. Ask a friend to tie the chain around your neck.

Snack stand

This is a great project to make for your birthday party table. Your guests can pick a snack from each tier. We have put cherries and muffins on the lower tiers, and long pretzels in the top pot.

trace around the feet pattern on page 30.

YOU WILL NEED

two large paper plates	red gift-wrap ribbon
one small paper plate	kitchen foil
scissors	foam pizza base
large plastic drink bottle	felt-tip pens
	tracing paper
three bathroom tissue tubes	pencil
	scrap paper
round candies	two see-through plastic cups and two smaller white plastic cups
puffed rice candies	
writing icing in different colors	

1 To make the base, first trace around the feet pattern on page 30. Transfer the tracing onto scrap paper following the instructions on page 5. Cut out the template, and lay it on a foam pizza base. Draw around the template, and cut out the shape.

2 Cover three bathroom tissue tubes with kitchen foil, fixing it with paper glue. These will make the "legs" for the snack stand.

3 Glue the three legs onto the foam feet base. Paint on toe nails using red writing icing. To make the columns in the middle of the snack stand, place a small cup inside a larger see-through cup. Push round candies into the gap between the two cups. Make two columns like this. Seal the gap with a squeeze of white icing.

4 Decorate a paper plate tier by punching four holes around the rim. Cut four pieces of red gift-wrap ribbon about 4in (10cm) long. Fold them in half, and push each loop upward through a hole. Then push the ribbon ends through the loops to tie them in place.

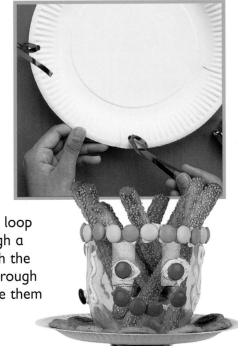

5 Stick puffed rice candies around the rim of the plate, using white icing. Then decorate a second large paper plate—we have squeezed dots of red writing icing around the rim.

6 Cut the base off a large plastic drink bottle to make the pot at the top. Make a face from candies, and stick them to the pot with icing. Now put the stand together: Glue a large paper plate on top of the foil legs, then a candy column upside down, then the next large paper plate, then the second column, then a small paper plate, and finally the pot at the top.

Glitter balloons

Make glamorous party balloons with glue, sponge stamps, and a sprinkle of glitter. You will need to hang up the balloons separately for a few hours to let the glue and glitter dry.

YOU WILL NEED

balloons	shiny gift-wrap ribbon
sponge	
felt-tip pen	glitter
scissors	newspaper or scrap paper
PVA glue	
paintbrush	

1 Cut a stamp out of a sponge. First draw the shape you want onto the sponge with a felt-tip pen, and then cut it out. We have made a star-shaped stamp.

10

2 Blow up a balloon, and tie a knot in the neck. Dip the stamp into PVA glue, and press it onto the balloon.

3 Hold the balloon over scrap paper or newspaper. Sprinkle gold glitter on the glue star. Shake off the extra glitter.

4 Use a paintbrush to paint on a glue spiral. Sprinkle purple glitter over the spiral. Remember that you can use the glitter that collects on the newspaper again—it will be multicolored and look lovely.

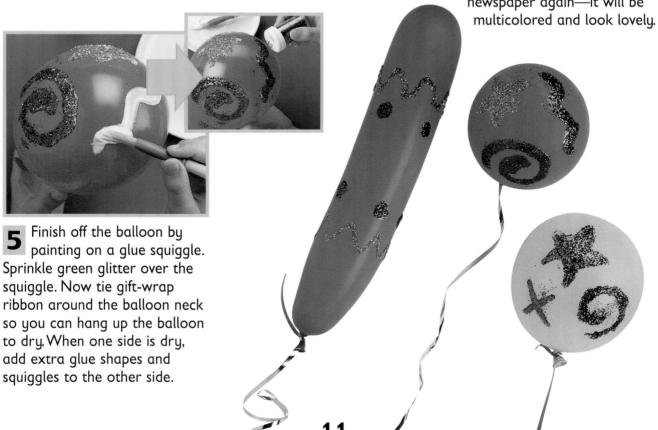

5 Finish off the balloon by painting on a glue squiggle. Sprinkle green glitter over the squiggle. Now tie gift-wrap ribbon around the balloon neck so you can hang up the balloon to dry. When one side is dry, add extra glue shapes and squiggles to the other side.

Cake slice box

Make a cake box for each friend at your party so they can take home a slice of birthday cake. There is a clever idea for going-home bags, too. Fill the bags with toys and candies as a parting gift.

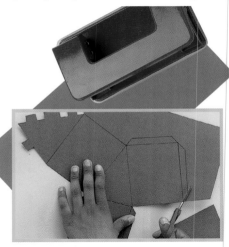

YOU WILL NEED

purple and green cardboard	scissors
	poster paint
tracing paper	sponge
pencil	glitter pens
ruler	red string
scrap paper	double-sided tape
small sandwich bags	hole punch
stapler	

1 Trace the cake box template on page 31. Use a ruler to draw the straight lines. Then transfer the tracing onto purple cardboard following the instructions on page 5. Cut out the shape. Cut the slits marked on the pattern.

2 Trace the candy on page 31. Transfer the tracing onto paper. Push the points of your scissors into the paper, and cut out the shape from inside to make a stencil. Place the stencil on the cake box. Dab paint over it using a small piece of sponge.

5 Thread two pieces of red string through the holes on either side. Leave them loose to make handles, and tie the ends together underneath the fold.

3 Add extra decoration to the cake box using glitter pens. Stick the sides of the box together using double-sided tape. Don't tape down the lid. Wrap a slice of birthday cake in a napkin, and put it inside. Close the lid using the tabs.

4 To make a going-home bag, fold a piece of green cardboard in half. Decorate it with candies in the same way as for the cake box. Punch two holes near the fold as shown.

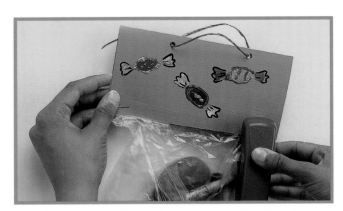

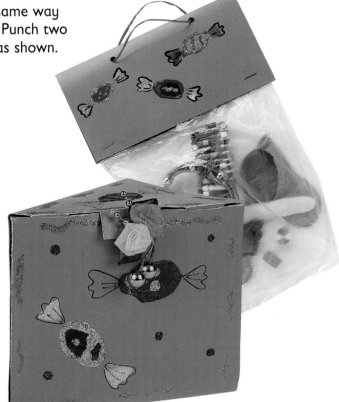

6 Fill up a small sandwich bag with gifts. Clamp the open top of the bag between the two pieces of cardboard, and staple the three layers together to keep the gifts inside.

Tumbler

This is a great way to give out prizes to your party guests. Fill the tumbler with *raffle tickets*, and spin it around. Roll up, roll up! Pick out a ticket from the tumbler, and the person with the matching ticket wins a prize.

YOU WILL NEED

cereal box	silver spray paint
scissors	
two small paper plates	cork cut into slices
two wooden skewers	scrap paper
poster paints	pencil
paintbrush	sponge
two boxes	firm cardboard
glue and ruler	double-sided tape

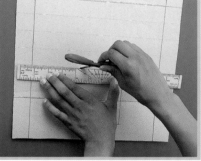

1 To make the barrel, cut down one side of a cereal box. Cut off the flaps at the top and bottom to make a flat rectangle. On the plain side, draw lines a ruler-width away from the edges down each long side. Use the blade of your scissors to score horizontal lines a ruler-width apart across the cardboard.

2 Near one short edge, cut a door flap in the cardboard. Now paint the whole piece in bright colors. We have cut a star shape out of scrap paper to use as a stencil.

14

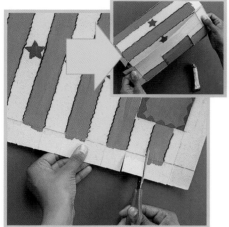

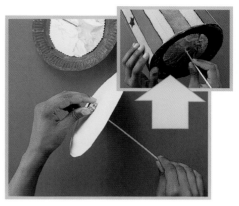

3 Cut snips along both long edges of the cardboard in line with the stripes. Roll the cardboard into a barrel, and glue it together.

4 The sides of the tumbler are two small paper plates. Draw around a plate onto paper, and cut out the circle. Fold the circle in half and then in half again. Place the paper circle on one plate, and use a pencil to make a dent where the two folds cross. This is the center. Find the center of the second plate in this way, too.

5 Make a hole in the center of each plate, and push in a wooden skewer. Glue the end of the skewer into a slice of cork. Decorate the plates, then glue them to the tabs at the sides of the barrel. Hold them in place while the glue dries.

6 Cut a strip from firm cardboard to make the base. Decorate it with silver spray paint. Choose two boxes to go on either end of the tumbler. Decorate them, and make holes in the sides at the same height. Hang the barrel between them by pushing the wooden skewers through the holes. Make sure the barrel is free to spin. Stick the boxes to the base using double-sided tape.

Memory book

Find a plain notebook, and turn it into a beautiful birthday memories book. You can stick in your birthday cards and photographs of your party, too.

1 To make the cake decoration for your book, cut an empty yogurt container in half as shown, and cut off the rim. Glue a piece of pink felt around the outside.

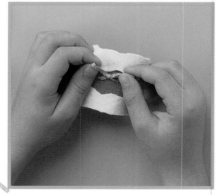

2 Cut two wiggly strips of white felt, and glue them to the top and bottom of the container to look like icing. Tie a bow in a thin piece of ribbon, and tie the ribbon around the middle of the cake.

YOU WILL NEED

notebook with hard cover	pink and white felt
patterned wrapping paper	thin ribbon
	tinsel
purple and pink paper	orange foil candy wrapper for flames
scissors	straws
pinking shears	small yogurt container
ruler	silver glitter pen
pencil	
candy wrappers	tinsel
glue	

16

3 Cut out a piece of patterned wrapping paper slightly smaller than the notebook. Glue it to the front cover. Now cut a rectangle of pink paper to go in the middle, a slightly smaller rectangle of purple paper, and a strip of purple paper for your name to go on the bottom. You can use pinking shears instead of scissors to get a zigzag edge. Glue the pieces onto the cover.

4 Glue the cake onto the cover. Then glue on pieces of colored straws for candles, and cut out flames from an orange foil wrapper. Glue them in place. Glue on a piece of tinsel to cover the bottoms of the straws.

5 To make bows for the corners, tie candy wrappers in the middle, and glue them on. Finish off by writing your name on the purple paper strip using a glitter pen.

17

Crazy cats

Show your friends where they are sitting for your birthday party with these crazy cats. Each one wraps around a cup and takes a sip of your drink!

YOU WILL NEED

thin white cardboard

thin colored cardboard for name tags

tracing paper

pencil

scissors

ruler

felt-tip pens

flexible straws

big cups

pinking shears

glitter pen

1 Trace the cat pattern on page 30. It is a half pattern, so flip over the tracing and trace again to make the whole shape. Go over the lines on one side with a pencil. Transfer it onto white cardboard following the instructions on page 5. Cut out and color the cat lightly and roughly to look like fur. Make one for each guest.

2 Use a second color to add details to each cat. Add whiskers and eyes and a border with a black felt-tip pen.

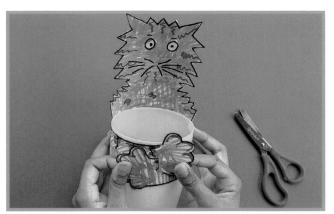

3 Wrap the cat around the rim of a cup, and mark where the two arms cross. Cut a slit in the bottom of one arm and the top of the other arm so you can fit the two together.

4 Cut out a rectangle of red cardboard using pinking shears. Write on the name of one of your guests with a glitter pen. Let the glitter dry. Cut a slit into the bottom of the name tag, and fit it onto a paw.

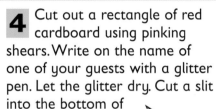

5 Make a small hole in the cat's whiskers using scissors. Put a straw in the cup, and poke the end through the hole. Now place the cups around the table ready for your party.

Splat invites

Have fun making a mess of your party invitations! You can write all the details—time, place, and fancy dress—on the clean back of the splatter invites.

YOU WILL NEED

- paper plates
- masking fluid or a white candle
- paintbrush
- poster paints
- old toothbrush
- gold glitter pen
- pencil
- scrap paper
- scissors
- straw

1 Write "Party" onto the middle of a paper plate using masking fluid. Let it dry completely. If you cannot find masking fluid in a craft shop, write it on with a white candle instead.

2 Paint over the center of the plate and the lettering using red poster paint. Don't go right to the edge of the plate.

20

3 Draw a splatter shape onto scrap paper, and cut it out. Place it over the lettering, and splatter paint around the edge of the template using an old toothbrush dipped in paint. We have splattered on blue, yellow, and red paint.

4 Thickly dab blue paint around the edge of the plate to make a messy border. Use a straw to blow the paint in toward the center. Leave the paint to dry.

5 To remove the masking fluid, rub your finger over the letters until a corner comes free, and then peel it off. Now you can see the word "Party" in white. Use a gold glitter pen to outline the splat shape. Write your invitation on the back of each plate, and give them to your friends.

 Bug muncher

This birthday party game is a bit like "pin the tail on the donkey." But in our game you feed bugs to the gruesome monster. Each player wears a blindfold and takes a turn to find the gaping jaws.

1 Let your imagination go crazy, and draw a mad monster with a huge mouth and lots of goggling eyes on stalks. When you have got it just right in pencil, go over the lines with a black felt-tip pen.

22

3 When you are happy with your bug, draw a few more the same size on yellow cardboard, and cut them out. Make one bug for each of your party guests. Stick a small blob of modeling clay onto each bug so you will be able to stick it onto the monster poster.

2 On a separate sheet of paper try out a few designs for some terrified bugs to feed to the monster.

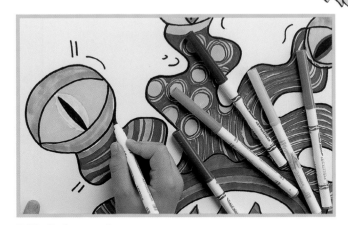

4 Color in the monster using thick, bright felt-tip pens. Ask an adult to attach the poster to the wall. Give each guest a bug, and take turns wearing the blindfold to try to stick your bugs into the monster's mouth.

Door knocker

Help party guests find your house with this ice-cream door knocker. Tie a bunch of balloons to the door, too, so your friends won't miss the party.

1 Trace the large cone pattern on page 31. It is a half pattern so flip over and trace again to make the whole shape. Transfer the pattern onto cardboard following the instructions on page 5. Score lines on the cardboard with scissors so that you can roll it into a cone. Attach it with tape.

YOU WILL NEED

two large paper plates

poster paints

tissue paper

string

bubblewrap

cardboard

tracing paper

pencil

ruler

tape

PVA glue

mixing bowl

paintbrush

rubber glove

two glass pebbles or real pebbles

scissors

strong clear glue

glitter

2 Make a second cardboard cone in the same way, by tracing the small cone shape on page 31. This will be the swirl of ice cream. Roll up bubblewrap, and wind it around the cone in a spiral. Tape it in place.

3 Glue the cones together to make the ice cream. Mix up half PVA glue and half water. Tear strips of tissue paper, and paste them over the ice-cream cone, using the glue mixture. Paste on three or four layers, and let them dry. Paint the ice cream, and sprinkle with glitter. Let the paint dry.

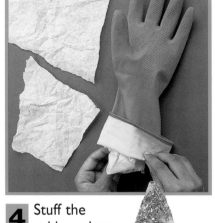

4 Stuff the rubber glove with scraps of tissue paper and bubble wrap. Don't fill the glove right to the top.

5 Paint a large paper plate blue, and make a hole near the center. Push the wrist of the rubber glove through the hole. Glue a second paper plate to the back. Tape a loop of string to the back near the top so you can hang up the door knocker.

6 Glue the fingers of the glove around the cone. Now glue a small pebble to the rim of the paper plate and one to the back of the cone so you can tap them against one another.

Magic dollar

Try out this trick at your birthday party. Slip a dollar bill under the ribbon cross. Close the book, swivel it around, open it again, and the dollar has moved to the uncrossed ribbons—magic!

1 Cut out four rectangles of cardboard, two red and two blue. They should measure 6½in x 3½in (16cm x 9cm). On one red piece draw a line 1in (2.5cm) from the bottom and another 1in (2.5cm) from the top. On the other red piece draw a line 2in (5cm) from the bottom and another line 2in (5cm) from the top. They are guidelines for the ribbons.

2 Turn the pieces of red cardboard over, and draw on wiggly borders using a gold pen. Decorate the blue pieces, too. We have drawn on lightning flashes with a gold pen and glitter pens.

3 Cut four pieces of ribbon 6in (15cm) long.

4 Lay the red rectangles face down so that the one with the lines farthest apart is on the left. Glue two ribbons to the rectangles as shown so the ribbons go underneath. The ribbons should be in line with the guidelines on the left.

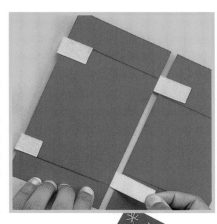

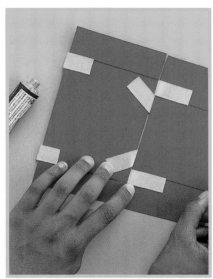

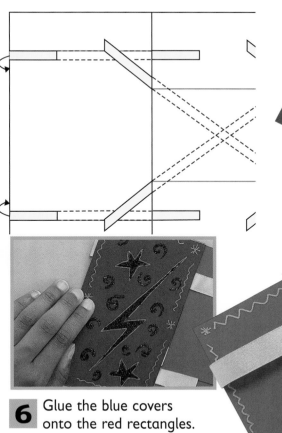

5 Make an "X" with the two leftover ribbons, and place them under the rectangle on the right. Glue down the ends over the guidelines on the right. Look at the diagram to help you. Dotted lines show where the ribbons go underneath the cardboard. Glue down the ribbons where they are colored on the diagram.

6 Glue the blue covers onto the red rectangles. Now turn over the trick, and slip a dollar bill under the cross.

Beaky birthday card

This weird, beaky creature makes a great birthday card. It is closed tight with velcro pads, and you can write your message inside the pop-open mouth.

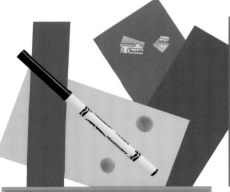

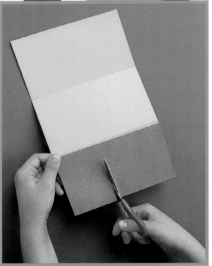

1 Fold the strip of yellow cardboard in half. Now fold it in half again. Unfold it, and fold in the flap on the right as shown. Cut a horizontal slit about 2in (5cm) long into this fold. It will be the beak.

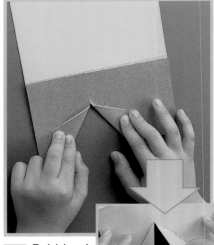

2 Fold back the flaps on either side of the slit. Open out the card and pull the beak forward, going over the folds again to help it "pop up."

28

3 Cut a piece of purple foam half as wide as the cardboard strip. Cut a wiggly fringe along one edge to make the creature's hair. Cut out two paws from blue craft foam.

4 Turn the card over, and glue on the purple hair as shown. Stick a square of velcro to each paw. Cut a small slit in the center of the card, and push one paw through, gluing it in place. Glue the other paw on the opposite edge of the card. Glue a piece of red paper onto the side that will be behind the beak.

5 Write a message on the red paper, so it will appear in the beaky mouth. Now fold the beak side over, and glue it down. Draw on big eyes with a black marker pen and glue on pompoms for pupils.

Patterns and stencils

Here are the patterns and stencils you will need to make some of the projects. To find out how to use patterns, follow the instructions in the "Making patterns" box on page 5. Some of the patterns are half patterns. There are instructions to help you use the half patterns in the steps for the project.

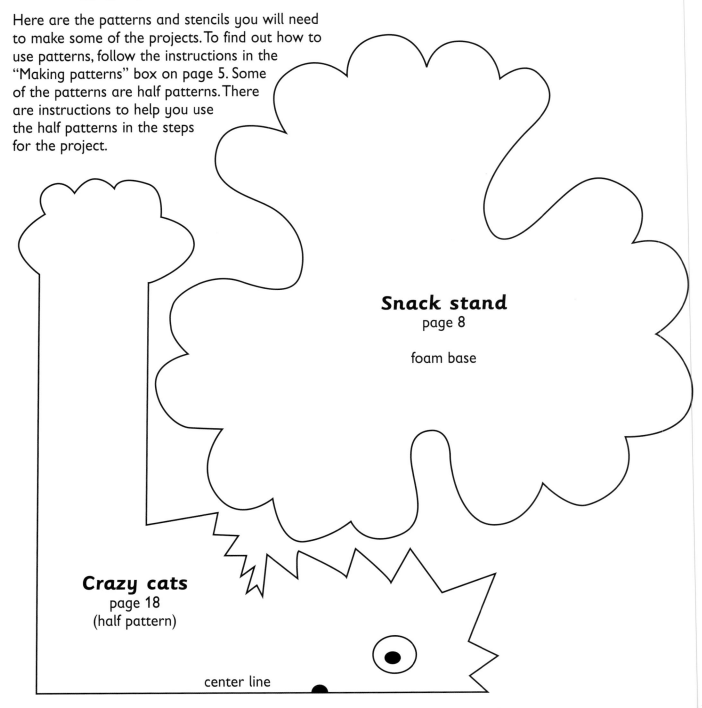

Snack stand
page 8

foam base

Crazy cats
page 18
(half pattern)

center line

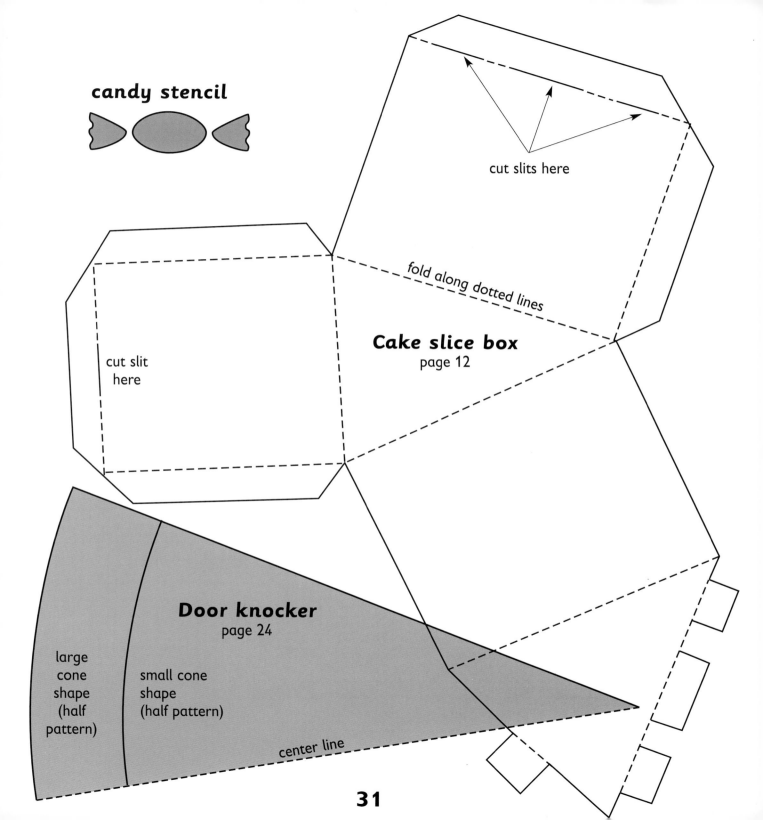

candy stencil

cut slits here

fold along dotted lines

Cake slice box
page 12

cut slit
here

Door knocker
page 24

large
cone
shape
(half
pattern)

small cone
shape
(half pattern)

center line

Glossary

gaping wide open and deep

glamorous decorated or dressed up in a stylish way

goggling rolling or bulging, usually describing eyes

gruesome frightening or shocking

pinking shears scissors with blades that cut zigzag edges in cloth

PVA glue one of the most common glues. "PVA" stands for polyvinyl acetate.

skewer a thin metal or wooden rod with a pointed end

stencil to apply a design to a surface using a pattern

template a pattern from which similar things can be made

tier any of a series of layers or levels placed one above the other

tumbler a rotating container for mixing, polishing, drying, or reducing something inside

Velcro a material of two strips, one consisting of hooks and the other consisting of loops, that fasten together

Index